This Vision Companion
belongs to:

_____

Who am I ?

_____

_____

_____

_____

_____

**TRANSFORMATION
CHURCH**

*"Re-Presenting God to the lost and found
for transformation in Christ"*

50 Scriptures
to Sharpen Your Vision

1 Corinthians 2:9-14	Hebrews 6:12
1st Chronicles 28:5	Isaiah 43-45
1st Corinthians 1:26-28	Isaiah 45:2-3
1st Peter 5:7	James 1:3-6
1st Samuel 10	James 2:26
2nd Timothy 2:7-8	Jeremiah 23:16
Acts 18:9-10	Jeremiah 29:11
Acts 2:38	John 10-10
Acts 5:3	Luke 5:3-5
Colossians 1:16	Mark 10:27
Daniel 7:13-14	Matthew 13:25-30
Deuteronomy 33: 27-29	Micah 6:8
Ephesians 1:11	Numbers 12:6
Ephesians 3:16-17	Numbers 13
Ezekiel 34: 25-30	Philippians 4:13
Galatians 5:16-25	Philippians 4:6
Galatians 5:5-6	Proverbs 29:18
Genesis 37:1-11	Psalms 139:23-24
Genesis 37:12-36	Psalms 16
Genesis 39	Psalms 23:5-6
Genesis 40-41	Psalms 5:3
Genesis 42-50	Psalms 96:1-4
Habakkuk 2:1-4	Revelation 21:7
Hebrew 11:3	Romans 1:21
Hebrews 12:2	Romans 10:17

Scriptures I want to remember:

_____	_____	_____	_____
_____	_____	_____	_____
_____	_____	_____	_____
_____	_____	_____	_____
_____	_____	_____	_____

The Circle of Faith

These are your Circles of Faith.
The outer circle is the Family God has given to you,
The second circle is the Friends you have chosen,
And the innermost circle has your Fighters - people who will go to war for you.

You are in the center, carrying the vision God has given to you.

Those who surround you must have the <u>crazy faith</u> needed to help carry your vision
Or you will have to fight your own people
From each of these circles
To bring your purpose to life.

- Pastor Michael Todd

Paste the Vision

Paste the Vision
(make it bigger)

"God created by imagination...so can you."

"See it in your mind; believe it in your heart."

"God can do the next best thing through you."

"Commit your visions to the Lord and He will establish them."

"Who will your vision inspire?"

"God has no lack of vision; He has lack of vessels."

"What is your vision for your future?"

"God is looking for people with vision to invest in."

"God will send your destiny helpers."

"Don't give up yet."

"With faith and patience you will receive the promise."

"Your purpose will put your passion to work."

"Your gifts were made for an appointed time."

"All work is pointless if God is not in it."

"God's plan for you is greater than the those you have imagined for yourself."

"Do not forfeit years of God's favor for moments of disobedience."

"*Trust in the Lord, and lean not to our own understanding.*"

"When your solution is not in submission to God's strategy, it is to your sabotage."

"How you wait affects how long you wait."

"Sow while you wait."

"Everything...even the thing you hate, is working for your good."

"The only thing worse than not waiting on God, is wishing you had."

"You were born for such a time as this."

"You will step into your prophetic calling today."

"Go out where it is deeper, and let down your net."

"Deny what you know and follow His instructions."

"The Holy Spirit will meet you there."

"There are certain doors that only God can unlock."

"There is a blessing waiting with your name on it."

"God does the dynamic in the deep."

"You will be able to speak to dying things and bring them back to life."

"God will use your life to do things that have never been done before."

"Everything He does has a grand design."

"You must give up control in the deep."

"Anchor your decisions in obedience."

"God will never lead you where He will not sustain you."

"He will direct you in the deep."

"He still wants you to move."

"While you wait, prepare your net."

"Let your net down again."

"Will you allow this situation develop you?"

"Everything good is doubled in the deep."

"You will change the destinies of those attached to you."

"Go loves you, but you need to love you."

"You are worth every desire of your heart."

"Your family will be restored greater."

"You are his masterpiece."

"With God, you will make the right decisions."

"Be careful who you talk to in your season of faith."

"You can lie, but not to God."

"Do not be deceitful with those sent to help you."

"Stop making excuses to not do what God has called you to do."

"You must perform in this next season."

"God has a plan for you; remove the distractions."

"Sacrifice anything that robs God of your attention."

"He welcomes you back."

"He calls you to lead."

"He will use you to rebuild and re-establish His temple."

"We are only afforded favor through His grace."

"He will meet you at your points of need."

"Your obedience will open doors of opportunity for you."

"God will finish what He started in your life."

"It is already finished."

"He hears and answers your prayers according to His will."

"With God, no evil is able to deny you of your blessing."

"Nothing sent to work against your success can prosper."

"He will increase your portion."

"Unless the Lord builds the house, it is all in vain."

"Miracles are working in your life."

"Separate yourself from your old life."

"Let go of what does not serve where God is taking you."

"He will do a new thing in your life."

"You will see the victory."

"Is God the main focus of your life?"

"Distractions make it hard to see what God is doing."

"What do you allow to consume you?"

"Your job is to believe; God's job is to make it happen."

"See it in your mind."

"Write the vision."

"Hope for it."

"Believe with crazy faith."

"Act like you already have it."

"Hope for more and go after it."

"Take the limits off."

"You have to see it before you see it."

"Faith is contagious."

"Envision your future; make the frame bigger."

"There is no limit to what God will do in your life."

"The steps of a righteous man are ordered by the Lord."

"Be thankful; do not become vain in your imagination."

"God does not bless who you pretend to be."

"Keep all eyes on God."

"Is your imagination taking you away from God?"

"Fantasy is fueled by the flesh."

"Anointed imagination is fueled by the spirit."

"Who is Lord over your life?"

"If it is birthed in deception, it is a fantasy."

"The good in you, will bring good to you."

"God is still good despite what you see."

"If it doesn't glorify God, it is a fantasy."

"If it doesn't produce the fruits of the spirit, it is a fantasy."

"You will be known by your fruits."

"God knows your imagination."

"His plans for you are always to prosper and never to harm you."

"Faith does not work for fantasies."

"Mark His words by faith, not facts."

"Vision is God's view for your life."

"Vision is visible."

"Vision is tangible."

"Vision is vocal."

"Vision has versions."

"Vision is vulnerable."

"Vision is your restraint."

"Where there is no vision, the people perish."

"A vision, without God, is just a good idea."

"Father, forgive them because they didn't see the vision."

"What vision has God given you to do?"

"For in Him, all things are created."

"Vision is God's investment."

"Vision is the vehicle between where you are and where you were called to be."

"God gives vision in the valley."

"God is the anchor; get anchored."

"The Lord promises to bless you."

"The only payment is patience."

"You are a sign of things to come."

"You no longer need to be afraid."

"...go without food as a way of worshiping me."

"I will save you and make you a blessing to them."

"Pray while you prepare."

"Get into the atmosphere of faith."

"Your full potential flourishes in the atmosphere of belief."

"The best time to kill a dream is when it is a seed."

"Some places most comfortable to you will kill your purpose."

"Whoever has your ear also has your faith."

"What has been feeding your spirit?"

"Who has your ear?"

"You must protect your ear to protect your destiny."

"God will speak it, confirm it and establish it."

"You were never meant to carry the vision alone."

"Where do you need to establish boundaries in your life?"

"You need family with crazy faith."

"You need friends with crazy faith."

"You need fighters with crazy faith."

"Godly friendships support your visions and feed your spirit."

"Who can you borrow faith from?"

"Will your people intercede for you?"

"Who fights for you when you are at your most vulnerable?"

"Who is talking to you and shaping your life?"

"What they say will affect what you see."

"God promised you an expected end."

"Play your part and reap in abundance."

"Do not allow those around you to deplete your faith."

"Ignore the bad report."

"They have never been to the land God has called you to occupy."

"Do not let their fear cripple your faith."

"Leading with feelings always spreads fear."

"Give all your fears to God, He will take care of you."

"What you receive in your spirit will determine how you respond."

"Avoid people who don't remind you of the promises of God."

"Belief is at the beginning of crazy faith."

"Even after all God has done...will you not believe?"

"Find people with enough faith for you to borrow."

"Who stands in the gap for you?"

"A different attitude creates a life of abundance."

"Speak it, and it will come to pass."

"When you complain about God's plan, He will take it away."

"God has ears too."

"Get into groups of faith so that you can flourish."

"Your circle of faith may become compromised; still hold on to God's promise for your life."

"The best way to get a crazy faith friend is to be one."

"Every No prepares you for a better Yes."

"Vision is valuable for your purpose."

"Without vision you cannot feed others."

"Vision is prepared from here, for there."

"God is still good despite what you see."

"We are saved by grace through faith."

"If it's not governed by the Word, it is going to be wild."

"Ask God to fill you with vision."

"It is already prepared; allow God in to show it to you."

"Vision is not valid until it is written down."

"The vision you have brings clarity to everyone around you."

"Who will be helped by the vision God has given to you?"

"May you receive endurance to outlast the doubt."

"Vision gives energy."

"Vision eliminates excuses."

"Vision illuminates exits."

"Vision frustrates the enemy."

"Vision produces endurance."

"See yourself telling your testimony."

"It's only crazy until it happens."

"Go out and live a transformed life."

I pray that the Lord will go before
you, make your crooked paths
straight and perfect your visions.

C.BOOTHE

FAITH HOPE LOVE PATIENCE FAITH HOPE

HOPE LOVE PATIENCE FAITH HOPE LOVE

LOVE PATIENCE FAITH HOPE LOVE PATIENCE

PATIENCE FAITH HOPE LOVE PATIENCE FAITH

FAITH HOPE LOVE PATIENCE FAITH HOPE

HOPE LOVE PATIENCE FAITH HOPE LOVE

LOVE PATIENCE FAITH HOPE LOVE PATIENCE

PATIENCE FAITH HOPE LOVE PATIENCE FAITH

FAITH HOPE LOVE PATIENCE FAITH HOPE

Made in the USA
Monee, IL
23 December 2021